'With gentle humour and self-effacing honesty, Di Castle charts the progress of Nanny-hood from the life-changing first phone call to the grandchild's teens. Sparing no blushes, these affectionate rhymes record the incidents and stages that all grandparents will recognise.'

Adrienne Dines

Creative Writing Tutor and author of *Toppling Miss April*
(published Transita 2005)

'The collection is both inspiring and intriguing (accompanied by delightful illustrations).'

Roderick Grant

Author of *Clap Hands For the Singing Molecatcher* and *Stathalder, A Highland Estate.*

'I LOVE Reluctant and Rules – made me laugh.'

Louise Gibney @MissWriteUK

Grandma's Poetry Book

A Collection of Poems
by Di Castle

Illustrated by
Denise A Horn

Matador
9 Priory Business Park,
Wistow Road, Kibworth Beauchamp,
Leicestershire. LE8 0RX
Tel: (+44) 116 279 2299
Fax: (+44) 116 279 2277
Email: books@troubador.co.uk
Web: www.troubador.co.uk/matador

ISBN 978 1784620 240

British Library Cataloguing in Publication Data.
A catalogue record for this book is available from the British Library.

Typeset in 11pt Aldine401 BT Roman by Troubador Publishing Ltd, Leicester, UK
Printed and bound by CPI Group (UK) Ltd, Croydon, CR0 4YY

Matador is an imprint of Troubador Publishing Ltd

For Amy, Erin, James, Tom, Sam, Eva and Rita

Poetry is nearer to vital truth than history.

Plato

How do poems grow? They grow out of your life.

Robert Penn Warren

Contents

Preface

As a child, I enjoyed A A Milne's poetry and later grew to love the humour and bouncy verse of Spike Milligan and Pam Ayres.

The Inspiration for *Grandma's Poetry Book* was the birth of my first grandchild, the huge, unexpected emotion galvanising my writing after a 'dry' spell. My notebooks began to fill with chance remarks and a few lines of verse, later honed and tweaked, entered into competitions and anthologies and even given to family on special occasions. 'Mother's Day' is one example of a poem sent in recognition of my daughter's first special day.

Some poems originated in a chance remark. The phrase 'We don't do that...' in *Rules,* for example, was said by a midwife. *Reluctant, No Stereotypes Please* and *All Change* arose from conversations with my friend, Jill, fifteen years ago. As with any writer, inspiration also arose from observation and eavesdropping other grandmothers and grandchildren.

Some scenes did happen although I have used creative licence for effect. *Behind the Curtain, The Imposter, Amy's Party* and *Babysitting* fall into this category. Other poems, such as *Mumbaba, Doubles* and *Schoolgirl,* were written to capture memorable experiences. *Closure* and *If You Could See Her Now* were written in memory of my mother-in-law. Both still make me shed a tear.

As the collection grew, I sought an illustrator who could

bring the poems to life. Denise fell in love with the poems and couldn't wait to start. Her enthusiasm and humour have been unfailing throughout the project.

Grandma's Poetry Book is a nostalgic childhood journey as seen through the eyes of a grandmother. The collection aims to capture the many facets of those fleeting easily forgotten moments. Some verses will make you smile or even laugh and some may make you cry. I hope you will enjoy reading them as much as I enjoyed writing them.

Di Castle

Reluctant

I've hit the town with my friend Mo.
We lost all sense of time.
Trying hats and drinking wine.
Laughing about our prime.

We both have adult children.
Now enjoy an empty-nest.
All our days are fancy-free.
Less work and ample rest.

But some friends talk of babies.
Their grandkids fill their days.
But us, we organise our lives
In liberated ways.

We like our freedom, can't believe
The ones who coo and crow,
Who say that being granny's best.
We just don't want to know!

We're both so glad that we're not *grannies*.
As we find that quite a few
Steer every conversation
To tell it *all* to you.

We're sure that once we've made the switch
We'll enter granny mode,
But then we'll spend life pushing
Prams and pushchairs up the road!

So *please* don't make us grandmothers!
For many a moon and day.
You kids have your careers these days.
Don't throw them all away.

Oh *please* don't make us grandmothers!
Well … not yet anyway.
We'd like more fun in fifties fling
Before it flies away.

No Stereotypes Please

Mo and I are walking, watching
Grandmas pushing swings,
Blowing bubbles, reciting rhymes,
Doing silly things.

We've both decided not to be
Typical grandmothers.
No matter what we see or hear
We *won't* be like the others!

We are reluctant grannies.
We enjoy life as it is.
Don't want routines and fun replaced
By living in a tizz!

We had the babes, brought up the kids
Now we deserve a rest.
Don't want our suspect talents
Put to offspring's test.

Our houses both have bits and bobs
Collected at boot sales.
We dread the day they're put up high
Amidst the screams and wails.

We like our junk food, fags and booze
But they would have to go.
Back to mashed potatoes
And making up play-doh.

No tipple on a Saturday.
We'd have to be alert.
When babysitting for the tot,
Bad language mustn't blurt.

But please don't pigeonhole us,
As if we're gifted with a gem,
Our hearts could turn full cycle
And we'd give our all to *them*.

One year BG

All Change

My friend, Mo, she phoned today.
She didn't have that much to say
On politics, the Queen and Di
Or those house prices booming high.

She gave the news in happy tone.
Enough to turn my brain to stone.
Her daughter has announced today
A first grandchild is on the way!

She's changed already, yes she has!
No more talk of razzmatazz!
She spoke of knitting, scans and prams
Not GM food or traffic jams.

No views on Tony Blair today.
My friend's mind has gone astray.
Her finance bent now runs amok.
Granny bonds not blue chip stock.

Her new career plan is no more.
It's baby mags she does adore.
Cosmopolitan's in the bin.
Bottles are out and breast is in.

No more shopping trips to plan.
Our business scheme flushed down the pan.
Now she's enrolled in Granny Classes
And forgot her A grade Science passes.

She's reading books on baby care,
Choosing gate for bottom stair.
Revising nursery rhymes and ditties,
What's more, it seems it's ME she pities!

So back to basics I must go.
Need someone NOW for London show.
No! Not a pantomime or Noddy!
Someone out there? Anybody!

Invisible

I knew before the letter dropped
That you were on your way!
Your mother wrote and told me.
I won't forget that day.

I knew before I read those words
'A granny you will be'
Your mother's eyes, looks so serene
Some changes I could see.

Cigarettes and alcohol
Were now well off the list.
No thanks to paté and soft cheese.
I quickly got the gist.

Your mother sent a card from you
To say 'Nan, see you soon'.
It won't be long before you're here.
Though I must wait till June.

I feel so old and ill-prepared
So before I shout hurray.
I've heard that things are not the same
As in your Nanny's day.

What!? No boiling nappies?
What? No carriage prams?
What? They sit in car seats?
What? They're weighed in grams?

We didn't have a Mothercare,
A Baby Gap or Next.
We laid them on their tummies
If they were rather vexed.

Perhaps I need to find a class
For first-time Grans who do
Have a blurry, furry memory
And need to learn what's new!

Certainly need some lessons
On how to set up pram.
I've seen Grans pull, push, click and twist,
Kick here, then BANG and WHAM.

Millennium Baby

Millennium Baby coming soon.
Should get some news tomorrow noon.
When new Dad phones, he's bound to say
The sex, the weight, the time of day.

Or so I thought, but should know better.
No details spilling to the letter.
'It's a girl,' he said, 'I'm pleased for you.
Now I must go, I've things to do.'

So when I drove through countryside
Big broad grin, my jaw stuck wide.
I worried, 'was the baby fine?'
He'd missed that most important line.

But happy Nanny, sunny day,
Driving down the motorway
Thinking while on automatic.
How our life is never static.

Wonder what you'll look like?
Pretty as your Mum?
Dark as Dad? Blonde like me?
Sweet as sugar plum?

Babies come and babies grow.
On loan they are until they go.
Can't be sure they'll do me proud,
But just for now, I'm on a cloud!

Live So Far

I live so far;
Must run a car
To see you grow,
And kisses blow.
Wish I lived somewhere near,
Then every day I'd come and peer.

Behind The Curtain

Just behind the curtain.
Just out of view.
My baby girl sits
Bedazzled by you!

'Go in,' says the nurse,
'I can see who you are!
Like mother, like daughter,
The baby's Grandma!'

I pull back the curtain,
See pink baby face
Holding a bundle
Of blankets and lace.

Heart lurches, head spins,
Mind whirls – how time flew!
Thirty years since I held her?
Like she's holding you.

Your mum looks at me,
Disbelief in her eyes.
'Can't believe that we made her,
Fingers, toes – tiny size.'

Wonder is catching,
I stand there transfixed.
Tears near to the surface,
Emotions are mixed.

She looks so vulnerable,
Naïve and new.
Young girl become mother
To adorable you.

Rules

We don't do this.
We don't do that.
We do it like this.
We do it like that.

What I'm always being told
Is my ideas are really *old*.
They do it all new-fangled ways
Not like my fuddy-duddy days.

They'll do it their way, that's quite clear.
Won't hurt my feelings, never fear.
One day, who knows, might come a plea
For more advice and they'll ask me!

After sleepless nights and tearful days,
Struggling through her 'new mum' haze,
She might be glad to try a phase
Back to my 'old fashioned' ways.

For now I'm saying nothing.
I'm going with my gut.
So as I coo and crow and nod
My lips stay tightly shut.

(an earlier version of this poem appeared in
Decanto Magazine in 2002)

By The Book

They went to classes on Birth and Baby,
Read the books and learnt the lot.
But in three weeks of parenthood
All this knowledge went to pot.

They phoned me up in great surprise.
This one, they said, just cries and cries.
No time to eat or have a bath,
Or read a book on this new path.

New mother was a real high flier.
Exams, degree, then yuppie buyer.
Got promoted, was the boss.
Her 'natural break', their greatest loss.

But now she never talks of shop
With tummy and her boobs a flop.
Where is the girl who did staff training
This baby's fairly done her brain in.

I phone and ask 'Now how are you?'
'We're fine,' she says, 'we've done a poo!'
'But how are you?' I ask again,
My daughter's really lost her brain.

Can't do this, can't do that,
All day long, I've been sat.
Working like a milk machine!
… and that last nappy was really green!

Is this my life for ever and ever?
Return to work? Oh never, EVER!
But without her work she's quite insane,
This new mum who's lost her brain.

Mistakes are rife, feeling blue.
The love affair that's worse when new.
First babies bring the means to err.
I know – I was the same with HER!

Des Res or Chez Mess

Dads are into DIY
But Mums just want to roam.
It's not much fun for mums and babes
To have to stay at home.

So Mummy goes to Monkeyworld
And Farmer Palmer's Place.
She's notching up the kiddie sights
As if she's in a race.

Poor Dad can't understand it.
Why can't they be content,
To stay home, play and make the tea?
He can't see why they went!

But remember, Nanny's wisdom
When clearing up the mess,
A happy, healthy, tired out baby
Is better than Des Res.

Babysitting

Babysitting is such fun.
It's then I feel like Number 1,
But baby has a different view.
Her look says, 'Strange this! Who are you?'
And then her mouth drops open wide
Emits a scream – I want to hide.
I utter soft, 'Tis only me!'
But all she wails is, 'WANT MUMMY!'

I try some rocking – cuddles too,
But still I get this loud 'boo hoo'.
A drink is downstairs, shall we go?
But bribes and treats are met with, 'No!'
What does she want, what does she say?
Perhaps a biscuit or some play?
Then just as I am getting tired,
I understand what is required.

The word's not 'finger', 'thing' or 'ring'.
She's not saying 'dink' but, oh dear, SING!
A song for Teddy, Mum and Nan
So must increase my memory span.
Order taken – deliver quick!
Top grade songs, in tune and slick!
So Rock-a-bye and This Old Man
Are dragged up by her doting Nan.

Time passes on – Babe's eyelids drooping.
Nanny now is tired and stooping.
To the door she's quietly creeping
But 'neath the eyelids Babe is peeping.
And … so it's Twinkle Little Star
With Nanny's eyelids drooping far.
Then 'more' is ordered from the tot.
Poor brain. The words have gone to pot.

When Mum and Dad come through the door,
Can't tell them how my pride is sore.
'She was no trouble. It was a ball!
She slept right through – didn't cry at all!'
…
For if I reveal my nerves are raw …
They might not ask me anymore!

My First Easter
or
My Chocoholic Mum

I may be only 10 months old;
I know more than they thinks.
I've watched as all my nannies, aunts,
Have come with bags and winks.

The bags all held large boxes
Shaped oval and with flaps,
With gaily coloured foil around
Some big boiled eggs, perhaps?

The bags got hid in Mummy's room,
I saw them – I was teething.
I screamed so hard they took me in
Because I act – 'Not Breathing!'

I peeped out from the covers
Saw one bag behind the door,
Open and half-eaten
Choccy bits upon the floor!

Denise A Horn.

I heard her on the telephone
Said she worried for my teeth,
But YES! Please buy her Easter Eggs.
Once a year would give no grief!

I saw her buy a big one
In a shop called W H Smith,
But then I saw her eat it ALL
And just leave cardboard pith.

I threw a temper tantrum;
I screamed and cried a lot,
But Mummy just kept looking
In my mouth and at my bot.

My Nanny knows what Mummy does;
I heard her tell her straight,
'I sure won't buy *her* Easter Eggs
For *you* to put on weight!'

So Nanny's bought a pretty doll;
I love it quite a bit,
But if she'd given Easter Eggs,
She'd be chart-topping hit.

And now it's Easter Day, hooray,
But all I got were socks.
Mum sat and ate my Easter Eggs
And gave me –
JUST THE BOX!

Second Chances – Special Times

Today's a very special day.
My favourite one you see.
I'm babysitting on my own.
Just Baby, toys and me.

No Mum to say, 'we don't do that'
Or to make the baby vexed;
Though, first when waving Mum 'goodbye'
The tot looks quite perplexed.

But soon we're playing on the floor
And making lots of mess,
Reading books and singing songs
And shouting 'No' and 'Yes'.

We put our hats and coats on,
For a trip to nearby park.
We look at cats and kittens
And hear some doggies bark.

We swing on swings and slide on slides.
We run and jump all day.
She makes it very clear to me
She likes her Nan to play.

All jobs at home are long forgotten.
Nothing matters more
Than tea and jammy bikkies
At twenty five past four.

I can't remember spending
Such magic hours as this,
Or getting such a thrill
From a splodgy jammy kiss.

My babes are grown, their wings have flown.
It's as if they never were
As tiny and so very sweet –
Their childhood is a blur.

But this is real and this is NOW.
I savour every second,
And if someone came between us two,
On me they haven't reckoned!

Busy Nanny

Who are these Nans who watch TV
In this twenty-first
century?

I swim each day, travel far and near.
Wear wet suit so I
Can swim all year.

Denise A. Horn.

I sing and dance, belong to clubs,
Use computer and cam,
Do video dubs.

I walk the dog and talk to all.
Then clear mud splashes
From the hall.

I visit grand kiddies, must be fair!
Return so tired
I sink in chair.

Programme begins, now what is this?
Loo…ks qui…te goo…d
Yaaawwwn, ziz, zizzzzzzz

Mother to Mother

On 10th of March 2002
I send this little rhyme to you.
To thank you in a special way
As we celebrate Mothers' Day.

This message comes right from the heart.
Through prayers and travel from the start,
From daughter, sister, girlfriend, lover,
You found yourself as Amy's mother.

Now you know a mother's pleasure
Interacting with her treasure –
Listening to each coo and sound.
Fun and laughter all around.

Motherhood is life's first-class,
As every day new milestones pass.
A special smile, a special word.
She's talking now – what's that you heard?

Those sleepless nights, the teething tears
Helping them dispel their fears.
The jabs, the spots, each dirty nappy,
So strange all this can make you happy!

But childhood passes in a flash,
As through our busy lives we dash,
To earn a crust, keep fit and feed,
Homework to do, books to read.

Mothers' Days will come round fast.
Quicker each year than those long past.
They send us in a reflective mood,
Gazing proudly on our brood.

So make the most of all those days –
Let her linger in childlike ways.
Remember she's on loan to you.
In God's great plan she's more to do.

First give her roots and wings she'll grow
And very soon before you know,
She'll fly the nest like you before,
And you'll not have her any more.

Career Nanny

These women who set all aside,
Go for career – will not be tied.
No time to 'be a Nanny' – shame!
Life's so short, can't miss the game.
For in our lives we have a choice
To do what makes our hearts rejoice.

I say 'I choose' to Nanny be,
For when I'm on my death bed, me …
Won't say I wish I'd spent more time,
Working for that extra dime.
I'll say, I'm glad I had the chance
To play on swings, to sing and dance!

No costly presents can I buy.
My bank account no longer high,
But time I have to spend on her
And feelings I'd long buried, stir.
I feel I'm back at 23.
We have such fun, she and me.

The inspiration for this poem came around 2003 from Linda Bellingham who said 'women have no time to be a granny, they are working for their pensions'

Career versus Babies

They're travelling countries far and wide.
No babies yet, they'd be too tied,
But now she's reaching 34
Her chances are not many more.

What will she do when stuck at home?
Still craving more to rove and roam?
I hope they'll then be needing me
A willing babysitter me!

So daughter travel wide and far
And take along your dear old Ma.
A built in babysitter, she
Will come along quite happily.

Tiny Times

To ride on steam train
Dig in sand

To be a lion
Hold tiny hand.

Testing Times

When Mummy does your nappy
You do a lot of kicking.
Naughty Nanny uses biscuits
To keep you busy licking.

You roll around and play the fool.
You drive your Mummy mad.
Isn't it a pity
That sometimes girls are bad?

You test your Mummy daily
To see how far she goes.
And then you do it all again
To keep her on her toes.

You stand in high chair, grin and stare.
Your Mummy stares you back.
Your little eyes show spirit.
Don't lose it with a smack.

She says 'sit down' and then says 'please'.
You laugh right in her face.
At 20 months you're canny now,
But need to know your place.

Sometimes you play up Mummy
To make a play at Dad.
You kick and hit and pull her hair
And make her very sad.

You think it's very funny
But I tell you that it's not.
But I can't bear to tell you off,
You're such a lovely tot.

Funny that when Mum and Dad
Are not around to test,
And Nanny is your minder,
Your behaviour is the best.

But when your Mum comes through the door
You change at once and how!
You show off then and cause a scene
Attention WANTED NOW!

Nanny's Day

You're getting very bossy
And like to show off some;
Especially when Nanny
On her special day, has come.

Last week we took you swimming
And you ran off from the booth.
Fear and tempers mounting!
Tension! Nanny soothe!

You had a little friend with you.
You both held hands – so sweet.
Sitting in your bathrobes,
Dan-g-ling your feet.

Others passed, said 'Ooh!' and 'Ahh!'
'Poppets! Aren't they sweet?'
Of course, they are, the dressing's done,
And chocolate is the treat.

Mummy's love ignores the bad
And praises up the good.
She's setting good examples.
Like I wish some others would!

She knows today and she knows why
You're driving her so wild.
It's all because your Nanny
Comes to see her dear grandchild.

Nothing Like a Granddaughter

There was once a time when life was grey.
One day seemed like another.
But then life changed when I became
A first-time proud grandmother!

There's nothing like a granddaughter
To brighten up your day.
Whatever's passed or come in post,
She has a sunny ray.

She bounds through door with much to say,
New shoes to show her Nan.
They flash, she says, and jumps about
To show me, 'see they can!'

And if she sees me thoughtful, sad,
She comes up to arm's reach,
Gives me a kiss, looks in my face,
Says 'We go to the beach?'

No matter what the day holds.
Dark clouds may hover near.
She has the knack to crank me up
Into a higher gear.

I recommend this Grandma role
To whom I speak and write.
My days are now a different hue –
Warm shades of light and bright.

And if you're favoured with a few,
Then trump card you've been dealt.
Add sugar, spice and all things nice
To feelings you have felt.

The Imposter

The first time I collected you
From nursery at 3.
Your mummy left a photograph
To prove that I was me.

I thought I'd wear my Sunday best
So wore my new fur hat,
Introduced myself politely,
Then waited on the mat.

The staff looked rather puzzled,
When you refused to chat.
But you just didn't know me.
You'd not seen me like that!

The staff were sure this was not Nan,
Not like her picture she.
But then I saw the picture
Did not flatter me.

So I took my hat and coat off.
Your face smiled so appealing.
The staff stopped dialling 999
To report me for child stealing.

Next time I went to nursery,
I wore my jeans and scarf.
I talked to all the mothers,
Letting off my raucous laugh.

No problem recognising then
Your Nan who came to call.
Now she was looking scruffy
And not speaking in posh drawl.

So here's a lesson from my plight
If you a Nanny are.
Just turn up in your old clothes.
Leave your teeth home in a jar!

And then you'll be so popular,
Your tot to you will run,
Throw arms around you, shout out 'Nan!'
Now who's the lucky one?

Amy's Party

So now you're two!
And look at you!
In dress so smart!
Smeared with jam tart.

So big! Now you can walk and talk
And run and jump and draw with chalk.
Seems yesterday that you were born,
Looking bored with gummy yawn.

This year you have a tiger cake.
So lucky that your mum can bake.
And everyone will want the eyes –
Jelly tots – the greatest prize.

All your friends are coming round
Boys and girls make lots of sound.
Floor will gleam with new squashed jelly
While world cup fans watch goals on telly.

Feet will grind the crisps to dust.
Hair will not look quite so fussed,
Glued up with sticky things unknown
And orange juice to heighten tone.

Some tears, no doubt, will add to joy
As terrible twos fight for each toy.
Sausages will roll on floor
And stick beneath the opened door.

So when your mum is on her knees,
Wiping cake and shouting 'Jees…'
Give her a kiss and say you 'luv 'er',
Because next year you'll want ANOTHER!

What's In A Name?

Nannies go by many names.
Some families sport a few.
They're either Nanny, Gran or Nan
Or Grandma, 'Her' or 'You'.

I am known as Nanny Wo Wo.
I'm the one who has a dog.
But if I lived in Holland
I might be Nanny Clog.

So glad I've given up the smoke
So I can't be Nanny Fags.
Must temper shopping habit
Or I might be Nanny Bags.

I've had to stop the whiskey,
So I can't be Nanny Booze.
I'm down to only twenty pairs,
So I can't be Nanny Shoes.

How well I do remember
My little shrunken Nan.
To us she was Small Grandma
The other one was Gran.

Grandad may be Pops or Gramps
But who cares what you're called?
When you've had the chance to be a bear
And round the garden crawled!

Four Sets of Grandparents

Four sets of grandparents.
What a lucky girl!
But Mum and Dad are not so sure.
Their minds are in a whirl.

It's such a nuisance Nanny's told,
With parents who divorce.
It's double visits every week
And four Great Grans, of course.

Four sets of grandparents.
What a lucky girl!
When mum was small, twas only one
Nanny's lap on which to curl.

Four sets of grandparents.
How will they be called?
Will all be known as 'Nanny'
Or other names be scrawled?

Four sets of grandparents –
Babysitters many.
Each arrive with treat in hand
As if you hadn't any!

Four sets of grandparents.
Presents quadrupled more.
Family party all together
With ever open door.

Babies bring all sides together.
Decades of war, now peace.
All are cooing, laughing, loving,
Love four times increased.

The Toyshop

We saw him through the window.
We saw him on a shelf.
We saw him in a box.
We knew you'd like him for yourself.

Sitting alone in his big yellow box,
Bright yellow helmet, bright yellow socks.
He looked so lonely, sitting there.
You reached up for the box with the cute little bear.

Bob said with a tear, 'All the others are bought.
No-one wants me; I'm the wrong sort.'
You picked him up and cuddled him tight.
Your cute little eyes shining bright.

I said, 'Put him back. You mustn't touch.'
You did as I said; didn't like it much.
I walked away, then had second thoughts.
Want ten out of ten. Don't want noughts!

So now that Bob is back in your arms,
They took off his tag so no more alarms.
What will I say? I'm getting quite fraught.
Can hear your Mum grumble, 'Now *what's* Nanny
bought?'

The Helmet

My mummy's bought a helmet
For when I'm on her bike.
She says I have to wear it,
Even when I'm on my trike.

My mummy took me for a ride
On Hayling Island's paths.
After that I kept my helmet on
To swim in swimming baths.

I wear it at the dinner table,
To church, the shops, to bed.
There is no way it can be forced
Away from Amy's head.

My mummy wants equality.
No dolls or prams, I think.
Then she bought a massive biking hat
In bright and shocking pink!

But I won't take my helmet off
Even when it's time for bed.
Whatever dress I'm wearing
The helmet's on my head.

I put it on a week ago
And since that day I've grown.
Now Mummy cannot get it off,
Oo, ouch, yuk, moan and groan.

But … while I have this helmet on
They cannot comb my hair.
Or wash it, dry it, curl it,
Or get it cut somewhere.

So I'm keeping on my helmet
Each day and every night.
And if I stay out in the sun
The pink might turn to white!

The Advent Calendar

Today I woke at half past seven
A voice beside me said,
'Nanny, nanny, wake up now
And please get out of bed!'

Denise A Horn.

I sink beneath the duvet
Pretending not to hear
But persistence is her middle name,
She repeats it very clear!

'I want to go and open up
My advent calendar
To see how many days are left,
If today's a sheep or star.'

Truth is behind each flap's a treat.
That's why she wants to peer.
A cho-co-late for every day
Til Christmas Day is here!

Click Click Clack Clack Burr

Today I phoned your Mummy
To say hello to her,
But all I got was click, click, clack
And then the dialling burr.

I rang again and still it went
Click, click, clack, clack, burr.
I rang again because now I was
Quite worried about her.

Next time the phone was lifted up,
I heard a voice go '…er'.
And then I heard this noise again
Click, click, clack, clack, burr.

Mummy phones me now and then,
On your progress we confer.
You raise your hands to be picked up
Click, click, clack, clack, burr.

It seems you now can answer phones
But do not say a word.
It's just you experimenting
With click, click, clack, clack, burr.

Denise Ann Horn.

But, today when I answered
A lovely word I heard.
'Nanny!' she said, pressing buttons.
Click, click, clack, clack, burr.

Christmas is Coming

Christmas is coming.
The money's getting thin.
But, must buy some biscuits
To put in Nanny's tin.

Christmas is coming.
Our birds the nest have flown.
But now they're breeding by the score.
Our family has grown.

We thought that when they flew away
Spare cash would fill the coffers,
But now the Christmas gifts are wrapped,
We live on special offers!

The goodies bought for number one
No longer are the fad.
How old is grandchild number three?
Asks quite confused Grandad.

We think we've got it right at last
For grandchild number four.
But what to get for number five
We really are not sure.

No Bob the Builder, Barbie Doll,
She's far too young for that.
Sweets are out and so's TV.
Oh … hmmm … What to give their cat?

Christmas is coming.
The kids will make a din,
And that is just the parents.
The child is sleeping in.

Christmas is coming.
We're off to shop again.
Cupboard's bare of headache pills
And … oh … don't forget the gin.

Christmas is coming.
I'll take it on the chin.
I'll spend it now … while waiting for
That elusive lottery win.

Christmas is coming.
I need that lottery win
To buy the food we'll never eat
That ends up in the bin!

Sssssssstimulation +++

In Grandma's day, babies slept
In prams and cots for hours.
But now Mums talk incessantly
Increasing sensory powers.

The rhymes are read, the songs are sung,
Nanny's ears are fit to burst,
For when it comes to animals –
Mum's noises are the worst!

I've had to learn to 'oink' and 'moo',
'Neigh' and 'woof' and 'squeeeeek'.
I've had to clap and shout 'Hurrah!'
At baby's loudest shriek.

The cleaner speaks in Spanish.
She learns French at nursery.
I'm singing songs in English,
Tri-lingual she will be!

But however much I sing them.
The words slip from my head.
Especially those tongue twisters
I tried today instead.

Now she is fast approaching two
She's learned Mum's repertoire.
So then when bedtime comes along
I'm pleased to say 'au revoir'.

Bombardment such as this, you'll say
Could get her in a muddle.
Why can't she put on baby's boots
And let her splash in puddle?

Oh, yes! She did! And in the park
A loud, flat voice did ring.
'Dr Foster went to Gloucester'
Pitter Patter. Sing!

So at dentist's, doctor's, waiting rooms,
Planes, buses, beach, BEWARE!
Forget your chance to sit and think.
You can't! The Mummy's there!

Drawing

Today you stopped me writing.
To make me draw a truck.
Then took my pen away from me
And on the page you struck.

꽏ꐤ.ꐤ.

'I drawing' you said happily,
Scribbling with glee.
Then told me that what you had drawn
Was Bob Builder's mate, Lofty.

We put on wheels and drew a man
Sitting in the cab.
Though Nanny cannot draw too well
You think it is quite fab.

So where's your lorry going?
Asked Nan, who's now Bees Knees.
Tot thought a while still scribbling,
Then cried, 'To Sainsbury's!'

Mumbaba

Today I rose at 6 o'clock,
Was on the road by seven.
One hour's drive so I can see
You in Mumbaba heaven.

Mums are sitting on the floor,
With babies in their laps.
No chance for Mum or Granny
To sneak some well-earned naps.

'Wind the Bobbin', 'Grand old Duke',
Now all sing 'Row the Boat'.
Nanny has to sing so much,
She gets a croaky throat.

Orange Teddy comes along,
To join Mumbaba rhymes.
Five little Speckled Frogs,
And other action mimes.

For one whole hour, your twenty friends
Are happy joining in.
Mums and Nannies proudly singing
To bring on toothy grin.

Then time for home, so off we go
With a 'Well Done' sticker stuck
On coat to show where we have been
Where others should have snuck.

In English towns and villages,
Mums and babies now are heard
Singing songs which teach the language,
Long-gone memories are stirred.

Doubles

One grandchild brings a heap of pleasure
So twins bestow double treasure.
We had a call at end of May –
Two little girls born today.

Denise Ann Horn .

Weighing just a few pounds each.
In care far from mother's reach.
Fed through nose – tubes like thread,
Incubator for a bed.
Nostrils size of needle eye.
Oh, please God don't let them die!

Little heads tomato size.
What a double first-class prize!
Born six weeks ahead of time
Bringing joy for a whole lifetime.

But fingers long and grip so tight,
Grabbing Grandad with such might.
Now here's a plus, as with December,
Two birthdays, but one date to remember!

Big Bunny, Little Finger

Now you're two.
You've grown so big.
Bigger sand pies
Can you dig.

No more Hedgehog★
A Bunny★★ you are
And now you open
Nanny's car!

But not so strong
To hold the door.
Bang! – your thumb
Is very sore.

Tears and cuddles!
Did you learn?
Nanny's warnings
Soon you spurn.

Now you have
More fingers squashed.
Oil and dirt off –
Must be washed.

Mind your fingers!
Hold up high!
How many times
Must we cry!

Mind your fingers!
Behind your back
Or that swing door
Will give you – Whack!

*Nursery class for age 3 months to 2 years
**Nursery Class for 2-4 years

Denise Ann Horn

Mirror Image

Some time ago was twenty years!
Went shopping, à la kids, no fears!
We shared the dressing rooms, no lies!
Same clothes, in turn, we took same size.

Then they were pre-adolescents,
My 32 was of the essence.
Aged 35 I had the figure
Without the stress of gym fit rigour.

Now I avoid those girly jaunts
For sad my figure looms and haunts.
The lines, the creases, flabs, the frump,
The sagging jaw, look down in dump.

My daughters boast of 8, 12, 10,
So I don't go out shopping, when
Their lithe and supple forms do frolic
To turn me into alcoholic.

Nice firm buttocks! Mine a splurge,
Enough to make a calm sea surge!
Small trim waist! Mine will expose
Between elastic skirt and hose.

Denise Horn.

Unknown the gene their busts are from.
Certainly didn't come from Mum.
But now I have them overtaken –
A view of 'down there' long forsaken.

But Mother Nature has a way!
What goes around, comes round they say.
Two figures are now looking slack,
It's time for me and my own back.

Hurray! They're pregnant, now I can
Go window shop, share room with clan.
So now I'm off on shopping spree.
Beside them I should look quite wee.

But hark! What's this? Oh what luck!
At baby clothes we now are stuck.
Prams and pushchairs, nappy sacks,
Tumble dry or airing racks?

'No need to try on clothes,' they say,
Until this baby's come to stay.
We'll wait til figure's back again,
You and I can clothes shop then!'

Sis

I've somehow lost a sister,
Since a mother she became.
We no longer talk the way we did.
It really is a shame!

We never get that sister time,
Just she and me – such fun!
Giggling in the early hours
About naughty deeds we'd done.

Swapping clothes, shopping fling.
Make up, boys, 'did he ring?'
We used to dance to latest bop,
Singing top ten – fit to drop.

Now I am out there on a wing
I never ever hear her sing
Save when she's humming 'rock a bye'
Lulling baby to 'shut eye'.

Oh Sis I'd love an hour with you
To tell you all the things I do.
Relationship and Career fare well.
It's Sis who's trapped beneath a spell.

Every time I see her now
I have to hear the when and how
Of baby's day and her routine,
New words heard. New skills seen.

I try to talk some sister talk.
Oh dear, the baby's dropped her fork.
Weaning, crawling, walking chat.
Reading now The Cat in Hat.

I'd like to see her once alone
Without her giving out a moan
Of how she's missing baby such.
This Motherhood is just too much!

Denise Horn.

Dankoo Fab

Your mummy says you think I'm great.
In fact you say I'm 'fab',
Which makes a change from daily sights
In mirrors full of flab.

Mum stops the car, then up my path
To Nanny's door she rushes.
A strangled hug will leave me with
A cheek of red hot flushes.

I think you like me cos I'm soft.
I do the things you say.
I sit down here and jump up there.
In Wendy House I play!

I can't refuse you, all demands
Are met. You're only two!
Who can resist this darling tot
Each time she says 'dankoo'.

Keeping Up Appearances

A simple walk there never is,
When you are at my side.
We have to go back to the park,
So you can have another ride.

You rush down slide, shout out loud!
'Nanny, come do it too!'
And then 'again', 'again' and 'more!'
Til I am all askew!

My hair is standing up on end.
My specs pop off my nose.
My knickers showing at my waist,
Boobs droop for pop-out shows!

My skirt now riding up my thighs,
My tights are sliding down.
I hope I don't meet those I know,
When walking back through town.

Now I sit in wooden train;
Am taken to a zoo
But realise I am sitting
In a pile of sticky goo!

89

Then we rush across the park;
It's free! We grab our chance
To sit astride a plastic horse,
Then gallop off to France!

The horse is wet and so am I.
My scarf has dropped in mud.
Leaning down, I wobble and fall,
Then land in a puddle, thud!

Now looking like the rag man,
I hear? Oh No! Four clicks!
Your Mum has got her camera out,
And taken more sick pics!!

Spoilt or What?

At Christmas time she had so much
From under tree and Santa's touch.
The whole of ELC was there
Spread from bed's end to top stair.

Now Nanny's budget feels the pinch.
Christmas prices made me flinch.
So I put away half I bought her
To save them for the second quarter.

When Easter and new baby come,
Distractions might be needed some.
So in my drawer I have dolls' clothes,
A dress-up mask with funny nose.

A microphone for Karaoke
So you can sing the Okey Cokey.
Then lead your friends in song and dance
And end up on the stage, perchance?

I've also got a magic slate
And brightly coloured plastic crate
But the chocolates I've put high and far,
Since messy advent calendar.

Closure

Switch on my mobile – click
Scroll
Menu – click
Select – click
Phone book – click
Select – click
One by one – click
Select – click
Scroll – Great Gran –
Options
Erase? click
Erase Great Gran? ok
Erased
No more!
Not ok.

Denise A. Horn.

If You Could See Her Now

If you could see her now
That granddaughter of yours,
You'd be so pleased
For that pregnant pause.

If you could see her now
Nurturing babe in her arms.
Gone the career girl.
Here now, mother's charms.

If you could see her now
With babe treasured and loved,
Taken all places
To carers not shoved.

If you could see her now
You'd revoke your decree –
That she'd not make a mother –
Too scatty, too free!

If you could see her now
You'd find it quite weird
And sad that you left
Before baby appeared.

Denise A. Horn.

But we believe that you can
Watch her and the child
And see her new ways –
Loving, tender, not wild.

And when we meet up
In the netherworld far,
I'll show you the photos
Proud Great Grand-mama!

Schoolgirl

Grey skirt, white blouse,
Blue cardy, striped tie,
Black shoes and white socks,
School bag, my oh my!!

My baby has grown.
Now look at her run,
From playground to classroom
Reception, such fun.

Transition from home to
This four-walled abyss.
Your life now has changed
With just one goodbye kiss.

This Nanny so proud
Outside classroom she'll wait.
Door opens, bright wide eyes
Teacher's new half-clean slate.

So 'what have you done?'
'Do you like it at school?'
The answer, is 'Nuffin,
I like it. It's *cool!*'

Denise Ann Horn.

'You must have done something,'
We ask during tea.
The answer is, 'Nuffin!
Don't keep asking me.'

'What did you do?'
I ask one more time.
The answer is, 'Nuffin,
But found slugs in some slime.'

'So what is the best part
Of school now?' I ask.
'The best bit is playtime
And making a mask.'

'I did some nice colours,
Some matching of 'fings.
My teacher's got long hair
And wears lots of rings.'

When you do nothing,
What can you see? …
'There is a drinks fountain.
Spurts water at me!'

New Baby (December 2002)

Mummy told me yesterday
A baby's coming here.
For a day or longer?
It wasn't very clear.

I wrote to Father Christmas
Asking for a baby sister.
I hope he's found the shops not shut
And hasn't gone and missed her!

I hope she doesn't cry all night
And keep me wide awake.
For if I get too tired and cross
Some meds I'll have to take.

I hope she doesn't take my toys
Or break my precious dolly.
I hope she doesn't eat my sweets
Or take bites out my lolly!

I hope she's not here *all the time.*
Just when I want to play.
Don't want a baby in the house
All day and every day!

Denise A. Horn.

Mum tells me it could be a boy.
A nasty little brother?
If that's so, I'll make her go
Exchange it for another!

So, if you're coming Father Christmas
And a sister you have got.
Please bring me one that's really nice
And leave her in the cot!

But if they have run out of girls
And only have a boy,
I'd rather that you brought instead
A nice big shiny toy!

Sibling Love

I've pinched him and prodded him
To make him go away,
But this little brother
Seems determined to stay.

So I'll push him and I'll pull him.
I'll give it all I've got.
A friend to this brother
Is something I'm not!

But years on, Nanny sees
When sweeties are around,
He'll give his last malteser
To his sister she has found!

The Computer Buff

So proud of my computer buff,
I know he's IT sound.
The web, email and internet.
Just look at what he's found!

And on the pitch each Sunday
Rugby talent I perceive
A winning streak, he is no freak.
Soon England, I believe?

And when it comes to Mathematics
None can match his skill.
He whizzes through his homework
Then skateboards down the hill.

James

Another trip to A and E.
Your Mum is in a state
First arms, then legs and now your head
Are destined to their fate.

See who's fallen in the pond
All wet, the tears are flowing.
Another bump is rising up.
Guess now where we are going?

Then upon the trampoline
You're springing very hard.
So high you fly right out the top
And bounce into the yard!

You never listen or recall
Safe ways and things to do.
But your cheeky smile makes my heart flip.
There aint much wrong with you!

Working

I had no time when you were young
To study, read and have some fun.
I missed your books, your knowledge too
Working, working all week through!

Working so the bills were paid
Houses bought, concrete laid.
Working for your trips abroad.
Working, working, never bored.

So now you've grown and I've grown old,
I've time to read and write I'm told.
To talk of culture, science new,
But you are working all week through.

Babies, jobs and you must be
All those things that made me, me!
Busy, buzzing, party cakes.
Working, working for all their sakes.

But what's this email from a child,
Doing Keystage newly styled?
'Some help is all I want from you,
As Mum is working all week through.'

Hurray! A project's here for me
For I have learned priority.
Now I can sit with him, while you
Are working, working all week through.

Then and Now

Ignorance was bliss,
No media in those days.
Families lived in happyland.
A constant rosy haze.

We didn't have the worry then
Of paedophiles and roads,
Drugs, foodscares and terror threat
Nor key stage learning loads.

Life was simple, hand to mouth,
No credit card to squeeze.
It was not the petrol fumes but coal
Produced the asthma wheeze.

No TV, cell, computer game,
Shoes shared – first up, best dressed.
And Cornwall was the only place
You were if you went west.

To be a Mum was slower then
But now they rush around,
So fast they cannot catch their tails.
They miss what's on the ground.

So give me back the 60s please,
I'm glad I had kids then.
60s mothers stayed at home
And men? – well, they were Men!

Brighton Babe (2010)

The smell of new born babies
On their hair and puckered skin.
Aroma that surrounds you
As you deeply breathe it in.

Long fingernails and lashes
Tiny pouting lips so sweet.
Eyes trying hard to focus.
These times are hard to beat.

Each day is full of wonder
As baby grows and thrives,
But life is never as it was
In your two lucky lives.

The first cry is ecstatic
But soon the thrills subside.
At 2am it's no delight
Till colic goes topside.

But remember when you're woken
In the darkest hours of night,
There are those who'd jump to take your place
And switch on baby's light.

They never hear the welcome sound
Of newborn baby cries,
And they never see the sparkle
In a baby's smiling eyes.

Fate does not make them parents,
For reasons hard to take,
And some have had and then have lost,
The child who used to wake.

So when you hold your tiny babe
And smell the newborn skin,
Be thankful that you have been blessed
The line of life is thin.

Denise Ann Horn.

Visit to Nanny (2011)

Biscuit in the plughole,
Nappy in the hall,
Toy train under carpet,
Whoops … trod on bouncy ball!

Never mind your hip Nan!
When can we have ice cream?
Now starts the competition
To make the loudest scream.

I haven't seen my newest specs,
In the dolls' house they may be.
Can you remember what you did with them?
Without them I can't see!

Pasta on the ceiling,
Carrot on the floor,
French bread in the keyhole.
Eeek! He's going out the door!

Bottle in the dog bed,
Door stop has been taken.
Now the door is closing fast.
Crash! The peace is shaken.

Lego in my winter boot,
Half-eaten apple too.
One whole roll of toilet paper
Soaking in the loo.

Nanny, how we love your soap,
It goes so gooey goo.
Squeezing Lizzie Arden,
We'll give a piece to you!

Mum has put the heating on
And lights are all switched on.
She's filled the bath up to the brim.
I'll mop up when they've gone!

Putlake Farm

We don't care if it's raining,
When you come to stay with me.
If wet, we get our coats and set
Off to the Farm. Yippee!

We feed the lambs
And ride the horse.
We hold the bunnies
Tight of course.

We feed the ducks
And chickens then,
Ride on the trailer
And back again.

We run and jump
Climb up, then drop.
Slide down the slides,
Til we're fit to drop.

Now where's Nanny?
Can you see her now?
She's stuck up there
On a plastic cow.

She's sliding down the cushion
And landing in the pit.
She's disappeared under the balls
Panting, red faced, so unfit!

Money, Money, Money

There was a time I bought a gift,
A doll, some Lego, what?
But now there's only one request,
Some money for the pot.

What about a brand new dress,
Some shoes, a DVD?
But no, there's only one request
Please Nanny, give money.

Here comes another birthday.
I'll have another try.
'I just want money,' again and again.
But me? I want to buy.

What happened to a pair of socks?
A pretty skirt to wear?
All they want are 'techy' toys,
To play with on the floor.

So tell me what you're saving for
With the money sent by me?
'An iPad, or a Kindle,
Or perhaps my own TV!'

Techy at Ten

So now you're ten!
Must look again.
How you've grown,
Now, your presents I'm shown.

'What's this?' I ask
This flat glass you had.
'Oh Nanny don't you know?
It's called an iPad.'

'We're getting Wi-Fi very soon,'
She tells me so I know.
I can see her on screen.
On Skype! Is that so?

'When you get an email,'
She says so patiently,
'You can write and tell me
All your news, don't you see.'

'I do write emails,'
I say right there and then.
'I'm really not that hopeless,
You Techy girl of TEN!'

Things They Say …

My windows look over Swanage Bay.
On sunny days it's clear all day.
In view is Bournemouth – just about
Enticing, always luring me out.

One day when Sam was only three
He came to fetch me saying, 'see!'
I held his hand, he took me there
To the window where he stood on a chair.

'Come, look Nanny, look out do!'
The sea mist now hid all the view.
I stood there with our fingers crossed,
'Look,' he said, 'the sea is lost!'

*****

What did Father Christmas have
For you in his sack?
'He left me sliplers and as well
Some binculars and a bell.'

Denise A. Horn.

One day we stopped at Corfe
To see the model village.
You told your friend
That you had seen … yes … a goggle billy!

Coming and Going

I'm waiting for your visit
In such a happy state.
Can't wait until I see you
Come barging through the gate.

Then it's noise and lots of laughs.
You certainly are a tonic!
But end of day, I have to say,
My headache's fairly chronic!

While it's wonderful to see you,
I love it when you come,
But home time can be better,
Just don't forget your drum!

Teenager

So now you're a teenager.
Thirteen yesterday.
Where have all the years gone?
Seems no more than a day!

You're taller than me.
I dwarf next to you.
Now on the computer,
Lots of tricks you can do.

It used to be a bucket
And spade on the beach,
But now it's your Kindle
You keep at arm's reach.

So glad you're still happy
To swim in the sea.
Especially the way
You love swimming with me.

So now it's get dry.
Hair put up in clips.
Then dressed smart and ready
For tea – fish and chips!

The Photo Album

When I became a Grandma,
Each Monday morn I took,
My latest photographs to work,
So all could have a look.

I was the first Grandmother,
The team had ever had
And so I thought that 40 pics
Should make them very glad.

Toddlers grew, then siblings came,
I took my leave and went.
And at my farewell party
A collection they had spent!

An album was their present.
Each face bore broad wide grin.
Their message on the card –
'*A book to keep them in*'!

Now we have reunions –
A meal and we all go.
But they are all grandmothers
With *their* own pics to show.

I'm up to five with more to come.
The gloss has gone I guess.
My photos are forgotten.
The ones I have, a mess!

But all their babes are new and clean,
Mine rarely fit for snapping.
So now they show *their* photographs
And *I* do all the clapping.

Index of first lines

Acknowledgements

A big thank you to all those who have patiently read or listened to this poetry over the years, especially Denise for proofreading, suggesting the occasional word and helping with punctuation as well as providing such fantastic, laugh-out-loud illustrations.

Thanks also go to Roderick Grant and Adrienne Dines for their encouragement in all aspects of my writing and for providing the initial reviews of this book. Also, to Louise Gibney for advice on formatting, her encouragement and social media tuition!

I would also like to thank the following businesses in Swanage, who, at the time of going to print, have agreed to hold book signings: Candleworld, Fi-Fi, Floribunda and York House Retirement Home. Also Gulliver's Bookshop, Wimborne.

Last but not least, I am so grateful to all my family, especially my seven grandchildren, who all provided the experiences needed to create this book. Thanks for all the laughs and for sharing your lives with me. You are all special.

References for companies and brands mentioned in these poems

www.mumbaba.co.uk
www.elc.co.uk
www.bobthebuilder.com
www.putlakeadventurefarm.com
www.monkeyworld.org

www.gap.co.uk/Baby
www.farmerpalmers.co.uk
www.sainsburys.co.uk
www.next.co.uk
www.barbie.com
www.elizabetharden.co.uk
www.whsmith.co.uk
www.lego.com
https://kindle.amazon.com
www.cosmopolitan-magazine.co.uk
Poetry quote –
http://www.brainyquote.com/quotes/topics/topic_poetry

Di Castle

Di Castle was born and bred in Hertfordshire. She always had a love of words and started writing as soon as she could hold a pen. After her youngest daughter went to school she began a career teaching in Further Education, while collecting a hoard of unfinished manuscripts. Later, her writing took precedence and, since becoming a regular attendee at the Winchester Writers' Conference, she has enjoyed success in their competitions gaining two first prizes and highly commended for articles on a range of subjects. She began writing Grandma's Poetry Book when her first grandchild was born in 2000. A few earlier versions of poems were published in poetry magazines.

Di enjoyed a nomadic existence in Oxfordshire, Hertfordshire, Middlesex and South Bucks before finally settling in Swanage in 2001. She lives close to her partner, Bryan, in a Victorian building overlooking Swanage Bay with views to Bournemouth and Old Harry Rocks. She has three daughters and seven grandchildren.

Grandma's Poetry Book is her first poetry collection.

Denise Horn

Denise Horn was born and bred in Yorkshire. As a child she always loved drawing and this continued into her teens, when she studied Art at the College of Ripon & York St. John. From there she went on to teach young children and enjoyed bringing the world of Art into their lives, enriching their art lessons by introducing mixed media and building their confidence in producing art work of a high standard. Denise moved from Yorkshire to Northampton when she married, and started a family, eventually moving to Swanage, Dorset, where she became a part of the large artist community. As a member of The Arts Club, she exhibits her bright, highly detailed paintings of the local area regularly.